Benjamin Franklin
on
The ART *of* EATING

SPECIAL LIMITED EDITION
to CELEBRATE *the*
275th ANNIVERSARY (1743–2018)
of the
AMERICAN PHILOSOPHICAL SOCIETY

WITH A NEW *and* UPDATED
FOREWORD *by* PATRICK SPERO,
LIBRARIAN *of the*
AMERICAN PHILOSOPHICAL SOCIETY

American Philosophical Society
Philadelphia • 2017

Foreword

Patrick Spero
Librarian, American Philosophical Society

Benjamin Franklin liked to eat. He liked to drink. He liked to entertain and be entertained.

Franklin also loved knowledge and was a great promoter of its advancement.

Lucky for Franklin, he lived in an era of sociability, a time in which the pursuit of knowledge, pleasure, and, yes, food were interwoven. The great salons of Paris in the late-eighteenth century, of which Franklin often participated, epitomized this culture, but these were simply a part of the intellectual life that defined the era. The growth of private clubs, voluntary associations, and charitable institutions throughout the eighteenth century all reflected this ethos. Franklin was a part of—and helped found—many of these types of organizations throughout his life. Indeed, Franklin's conviviality helped him become the towering intellectual he was.

Franklin's first forays into public service were premised on the idea that knowledge is best pursued in the company of others. When Franklin started out as a printer in Philadelphia, he realized that the ambitious young artisans who were flocking to the city had enormous creative potential, but he feared that competition or, worse, isolation would stunt the intellectual growth of his generation. He thus formed the Junto, a club of intelligent young artisans who desired learned camaraderie.

The Junto fostered fellowship by meeting regularly over drinks and dinner to discuss a wide range of issues. Sometimes they would discuss local business affairs, other times politics. But the Junto did more than just debate the immediately practical and pragmatic. Franklin knew many of his peers also possessed hungry minds that needed nourishment, so they also shared books.

As the Junto grew larger and more sophisticated, so too did Franklin's own thinking about the city's needs. He worried that the high price of good books imported from England made their purchase difficult for all but the wealthiest. Franklin saw this inaccessibility as a problem for the city as well as the individual. Without broad access to important books on politics, philosophy, law, and literature, the works that lay the foundation for a robust civil society, the aspiring middle class would be unable to realize their full potential and Philadelphia's growth would be stifled.

And so Franklin founded the Library Company of Philadelphia, a lending library supported through subscriptions to provide Philadelphians with access to a diverse and humanistic library. His aim, again, was not simply to acquire the most practical books. Instead, Franklin realized that a broadly educated citizenry was necessary to promote the public good and encourage economic prosperity. The founding of this lending library, which went largely unremarked at the time, was perhaps the greatest attempt to democratize knowledge in the British Empire up to that point.

The zenith of Franklin's efforts to advance knowledge came in 1743, when he founded the American Philosophical Society. Through his own travels and correspondence with far-flung contacts, Franklin realized that Great Britain's North American colonies, once a series of fledgling and isolated outposts dotting the Atlantic coastline, had achieved a level of stability and growth that would allow them to act with greater coordination. He decided that the now thriving colonies needed an organization that would serve as a central node connecting the leading thinkers with one another. By facilitating the exchange of ideas among the intellectual elite of the colonies, this institution would promote the advancement of knowledge, which would, in turn, enhance life for all colonists as these civically engaged members applied their new learning to their local settings.

Franklin published a broadside in 1743 calling for the formation of this organization. Named the American Philosophical Society, he said its mission was to promote useful knowledge. Franklin's thinking was surely influenced by his experience with the Junto and Library Company but his vision was grander in scope and inspired by his exposure to the learned societies in Europe.

His proposal consisted of five main ideas, all of which focused on cultivating a sense of intellectual camaraderie and many of which replicated the operations of the Royal Society in London.

First, the Society would consist of an elective membership composed of individuals who had made significant contributions in their respective fields of study and whose broader interests and collegiality would create a spirit of fellowship among this extended network of intellectuals—the "Virtuosi," as Franklin called them in his proposal.

He also proposed regular meetings for members at which ideas and correspondence could be shared, discussed, and debated in an open atmosphere of mutual learning.

Franklin wanted these exchanges of ideas to reach beyond Philadelphia and the colonies, however. He thus planned for the Society to disseminate its proceedings through what he called a "constant correspondence" among members and through official correspondence with institutional peers throughout the world.

The Society was also to encourage new research by underwriting experiments deemed worthy of investigation by the members.

Finally, he set Philadelphia as the headquarters for this new institution, believing a centrally located city would serve as the best repository for the material the Society produced.

These programs would form the heart of a society of intellectuals that would by its very existence and operation promote the advancement of knowledge. And, while the membership was drawn largely from the colonies, Franklin's vision was much larger. He hoped that the American Philosophical Society in Philadelphia would be a part of a transatlantic intellectual community in which scholarship was shared freely and new knowledge was constructed through collaboration and experimentation.

Franklin's vision was realized in his own time, and, to this day, the Society continues to serve Franklin's original mission.

The Society maintains an active membership composed of the country's leading intellectuals who are distinguished by having made important contributions in their respective fields. In the spirit of Franklin's support for intellectual diversity, the Society's membership roll books contain an eclectic list of scientists, humanists, artists, and civic leaders.

The Society also actively supports the pursuit of new knowledge through a robust grants and fellowships program that sends scholars out into the field to conduct research and brings others to Philadelphia to work in the Society's Library.

The Society maintains the longest continuously operating scholarly publications program in North America, which now includes digital components, and serves as the Society's primary means for communicating its work to the rest of the world.

The Society's Library continues to be a repository of knowledge, holding over 250,000 books and 13 million pages of manuscript materials.

The Society also shares its contents with the wider world through a museum whose exhibits inspire a love of learning in a younger generation.

Finally, the Society still hosts regular meetings, which are now major international conferences in which leading researchers in a wide array of fields present cutting edge research to an audience composed of some of the world's smartest minds. And, of course, in true Franklin fashion, these conversations continue over drinks and food following the official proceedings. The Society's founder would be pleased to know that some of the most engaging and productive discussions at Society meetings often happen around a table.

The Society thus continues to serve its lofty mission of promoting the advancement of knowledge through collaboration and collegiality. Indeed, what was a hallmark of Franklin's life continues just as vibrantly in the twenty-first century, if not more so.

It is fitting, then, that on the 275th anniversary of the Society's founding, it is republishing *The Art of Eating*. First published in 1958, the text begins with a wonderful profile of Franklin and his relationship to food by historian Gilbert Chinard. It is followed by a compilation of recipes and witticisms about food and drink that were found in Franklin's papers, most of which reside in original form in the Society's vault.

So prepare yourself for some sumptuous reading, and don't forget that, as Poor Richard once advised, a good diet "preserves the memory," "helps the understanding," and "makes us happy in this world."

Enjoy,
Patrick

BENJAMIN FRANKLIN
on
The ART *of* EATING

Preparing of Food is a greater Art and Mystery than many House-wives and others do think; and if it be well and properly performed, it adds much to the preservation of *Health* both of *Body* and *Mind*, for every thing has Power to awaken its Simile in the Body.—THOMAS TRYON, *The Way to Long Life and Happiness*, London, 1691, p. 92.

"Eat few Suppers, and you'll need few Medicines"—POOR RICHARD for 1742

Benjamin Franklin
on the ART of EATING
together with the
Rules of HEALTH and *Long Life*
and the
Rules to find out a fit Measure
of Meat and Drink

WITH SEVERAL RECIPES

American Philosophical Society

Copyright © 1958 by American Philosophical Society
L.C. Card No. 58-10724

Printed in the United States of America

Printed 1958 by Princeton University Press
&
Reprinted 1980 by Eastern Ligthographing Corp.

Benjamin Franklin
On the Art of Eating

THE accidental discovery in the Franklin Papers of a set of cooking recipes and the many allusions to food scattered through Franklin's various works and letters have led to an inquiry the results of which, however incomplete, may throw some new light on a little studied aspect of the Sage of Philadelphia. This unpretentious essay will not upset any of the established notions entertained on his way of living; it will at most add a few traits to the multitudinous facets of this uncommon man whose singular merit was to exemplify many of the virtues and some of the weaknesses of the common man.

Dr. Franklin, despite the accusations of "Madame la Goute," was neither "a glutton nor a tippler." He was a man who liked his food and his drink and did not care over much for sophisticated cooking. He was also a man endowed with an insatiable curiosity. "This is an age of experiment," said he once and, as a practical philosopher, he believed that the essential needs of man were not unworthy of his attention. In his essay on *The Principles of Trade*, March 1774, he briefly listed these essential needs: "Now things of real use can only be meat, drink, clothing, fuel and habitation."

His contribution to the systematic study of the last three articles is well known. His drinking songs have often been mentioned by his biographers and perhaps should not be taken too literally. It does not seem that his interest in food has aroused the same curiosity. When a young man he had practiced the *Art of speaking* of the Messieurs de Port-Royal, later in life he projected an *Art of Virtue*; we made bold to assume that, had he been able to put together and to systematize the many observations and notations on the subject which he enjoyed making through his whole life, he would not have objected to the title of this essay consisting for the most part of direct quotations.

THE EARLY YEARS

His early education did not prepare him for the noble art of gastronomy. Simple food was served at the family table:

"Little or no notice was ever taken of what related to the victuals on the table; whether it was well or ill dressed, in or out of season, of good or bad flavour, preferable or inferior to this or that other things of the kind, so that I was bro't up in such perfect inattention to those matters as to be quite indifferent what kind of food was set before me, and so unobservant of it, that to this day if I am asked I can scarce tell a few hours after dinner what I dined upon. This has been a convenience to me in travelling, where my companions have been sometimes very unhappy for want of a suitable gratification of their more delicate, because better instructed, tastes and appetites" (*Autobiography*, Smyth ed., I, 235).

Perhaps so, but we shall have occasion to see that this professed indifference to food calls for some qualifications. It is well to remember also that an active conversation was carried out at the family table and that friends and neighbors were often brought in by Franklin's father. At an early age Franklin was at least "instructed" to consider meals as a social function and, as often as he could, he kept up this pleasant tradition.

The demon of experimentation which possessed him even at an early age made him depart from this philosophical detachment. According to his own account, he was about 16 years of age when he met "with a book written by one Tryon, recommending a vegetable diet." He determined to go into it and got himself "acquainted with Tryon's manner of preparing some dishes, boiling potatoes or rice, making hasty pudding and a few others." When not cooking himself he was content with "a biskit or a slice of bread, a handful of raisins or a tart from the pastry-cook's and a glass of water."

When boarding with Keimer in Philadelphia, he was too busy in the printing shop to do any cooking, but he managed to observe faithfully the vegetarian precepts: "We had our victuals dressed and brought to us regularly by a woman in the neighborhood, who had from me a list of forty dishes, to be prepar'd for us at different times, in all of which there was neither fish, flesh, nor fowl, suited me the better at that time from the cheapness of it not costing us above eighteen pence sterling per week."

Yet he was not a fanatic: he had fallen from grace not long since when going by boat from Boston to

New York. On the way they caught fish: "when this came out of the frying pan, it smelt admirably good" and he made a great discovery, that since fish eat fish, "I don't see why I may not eat you."

When in London, however, out of necessity as much as out of virtue, he was very abstemious. When he visited his landlady at night, "our supper was only half an anchovy each, on a very little strip of bread and butter and half a pint of ale between us; but the entertainment was in her conversation." His breakfast was no less frugal. While his companions in the printing shop ate a "muddling breakfast of beer, bread and cheese," he had from a neighboring house "a large porringer of hot water gruel sprinkled with pepper, crumb'd with bread and a bit of butter in it for the price of a pint of beer, wiz. three half pence" (*Autobiography*, Smyth, I, 282).

Such is briefly the account given by Franklin of his experiment in vegetarianism. It is very likely that, when he wrote it, the many other experiments with food and drink he had indulged in had somewhat befogged his memory.

The story he told to abbé de la Roche and indeed to his French friends is slightly different. To them he did not make any mention of Tryon. He would have determined to follow a strictly vegetarian diet after chancing upon a volume of Plutarch against the use of animal flesh (Proceedings of the American Philosophical Society, vol. 94, No. 3, p. 218, 1950). As a point of fact, he could have found the most impressive part of Plutarch's declamation in a treatise published in London in 1724, by a then well-known physician, Dr. George Cheyne's *Essay on Health and Long Life*. To make the puzzle more complicated, it is quite certain that Tryon made use of Plutarch's text without mentioning his name. However the case may be, the work of Thomas Tryon deserved under the pen of Franklin much more than a casual reference. The title of the book, *The Way to Health, Long Life and Happiness: Or, A Discourse on Temperance*, London, second edition, 1691, somehow sounds familiar and should have aroused the curiosity of the biographers of Franklin.

There is much more in Tryon's treatise than an apology of vegetarianism. The author, who claimed only the modest title of "student of Physick," proposed a real philosophy of eating based upon physical, metaphysical and religious principles and systematically developed, "The like never before published." He started with a description of "four grand qualities whence the four complexions proceed," namely the bitter, the sweet, the sour and the salty or astringent qualities, establishing a "harmony" between them and the "cholerick," "phlegmatic," "sanguine and melancholy complexions." Long before Cabanis he disserted on the effect of food on the moral dispositions. His condemnation of the use of flesh rested on the assumption "that the common eating thereof awakens the wrathful Nature in Mankind (p. 249), and is at the source of wars." If he is remembered at all by the students of the history of ideas, it is because of his imitation and elaboration of the declamation of Plutarch in which he gave the piteous laments of the animals abused and mistreated by man: "The Voice of the Dumb, or the Complaints of the Creatures, expostulating with Man, touching the cruel usages they suffer from him" (chap. XV), with the Complaint of the Cows and Oxen, the Sheep's Complaint and "the Horses complaint against their Master."

Tryon was too good a student of human nature to believe that, after eating flesh for countless generations, people would radically change their customs. At least they could be instructed "in the least harmful way to prepare and use the flesh of animals." Thereupon, Tryon launched upon an elaborate discussion of the most natural way of preparing food, "wiz. Boyling, Roasting, Baking, Stewing, Frying and Broyling of Flesh and other food." Cooking with him is a science and an art and the different elements entering in the composition of a dish must be blended "even as a skillful *Musicaner* composeth a harmonious comfort into the variety of parts or as by skill tunes his Instrument." And again, "Cooks ought to be as skillful as Painters in their Mixtures, which if well observed, most people would be free from desiring such compounded Dishes" (p. 170).

A search, perhaps incomplete, has failed to reveal the forty dishes proposed by Franklin to his landlady and any special recipe for cooking rice. The list of vegetables is rudimentary, including wheat, barley, rye, pease or beans, kidney or French beans, "herbs raw or boyled," "colworts, cabbage and colly flowers," turnips, the best of all vegetables, equalled only by carrots and parsnips. Tryon did not give any detailed instructions on the preparation of food; he simply recommended to avoid fried meat and fish at all cost and to boil the vegetables in plenty of water.

In Tryon, however, Franklin discovered more than a practical cook book. He was probably indebted to him for the title of his essay on *The Way to Wealth* which echoes *The Way to Health.* More specifically he found in the book of the "student Physick" most of the principles and precepts listed in two pieces printed in *Poor Richard's Almanach* for 1742. The first one, entitled "Rules of Health and Long Life, and to Preserve from Malignant fevers and sicknesses in general," has been reprinted by the editors of Franklin's works. The second, "Rules to find out a fit measure of meat and drink" has been generally left out for reasons which remain mysterious. Both of them were certainly inspired by Tryon. If we had no other clue, the pious note with which they end would suffice to direct the reader to the original source.

Both of them are revealing: they express in a condensed form what might be called the intellectual hygiene of Benjamin Franklin. They deserve a detailed study which cannot be undertaken here. They have been reprinted as a fit introduction to the recipes.

POOR RICHARD'S ALMANACHS

The philosophy of the *Way to Health* permeates *Poor Richard's Almanach*. It is a worldly wisdom which does not preach abstinence but moderation, for we know that, "A full Belly is the Mother of all Evil" (1743), that "A full Belly makes a dull Brain" (1758), or as expressed in a more dignified style, that "The Muses starve in a Cook's Shop" (1758). If space did not forbid, one could quote almost endlessly from the sayings of Poor Richard. His precepts may be summed up in a recommendation which Franklin did not always observe, "Be temperate in Wine, in eating, Girls, and Sloth, or the Gout will sieze you and plague you both" (1734). This is the essence of the well-known table of

"Moral virtues" given in the *Autobiography*.

It must be admitted that he had also other masters. Despite Tryon's absolute condemnation of "Punch," Franklin inserted in the *Almanach* for 1737 a pleasant recipe for the damnable concoction (June 1737):

> Boy, bring a bowl of China here,
> Fill it with water cool and clear;
> Decanter with Jamaica ripe,
> And spoon of silver, clean and bright,
> Sugar twice-fin'd in pieces cut,
> Knife, sive, and glass in order put,
> Bring forth the fragrant fruit, and then
> We're happy till the clock strikes ten.

In 1743, he gave a "Method for making wine of the grapes which grow wild in our Woods, so that they may furnish themselves with a wholesome, sprightly Claret, which will keep for several years and is not inferior to that which passeth for *French* Claret" (Preface).

In practice, he accommodated Tryon to the general trends of the time and to his own dispositions. We know that the discussions of the Junto were enlivened and timed by a proper amount of wine, and that Franklin composed several drinking songs often mentioned and quoted by his biographers. But all this did not make him a "tippler," and he always remembered the first precept of his list of virtues: "Eat not to dullness. Drink not to elevation." He had seen too often the effects of heavy drinking not to abhor it. He was saddened when his friend Collins acquired the habit of "sotting with brandy." On many other occasions he had the opportunity to observe that drink and business do not mix.

When sent to Governor George Clinton of New York to obtain some cannon for the Pennsylvania militia, he recalled that the Governor first refused absolutely to grant the request. Then, "at dinner where there was great drinking of Madeira wine, as the custom of the place was, he softened by degrees, and said that he would lend us six. After a few more bumpers he advanced to ten; and at length he very good-naturedly conceded eighteen" (*Autobiography*, p. 363).

No less striking was the lesson, when the new Governor, Captain Denny, presented to Franklin the gold medal of the Royal Society: "After making liberal use of a decanter of Madeira wine, he became more profuse in his sollicitations and promises. He went even farther than he had a right to" (*Autobiography*, p. 422). He had a similar experience with Lord Clare from the Board of Trade, in London, in 1768: "He gave me a great deal of flummery; saying, that though at my Examination I answered some of his questions a little too pertly, yet he liked me, from that day, for the spirit I showed in defence of my country; and at parting, after we had drank a bottle and a half of claret each, he hugged and kissed me, protesting he never in his life met with a man he was so much in love with" (To William Franklin, Smyth, V, 147).

Franklin was too wise to be taken in by such effusions and not to remember that in business, in politics and diplomacy, temperance "procures that coolness of head which is so necessary where constant vigilance is to be kept up" (*Autobiography*, p. 327). He had also observed the evil effects of strong drink on the natives and concluded that, "If it be the design of Providence to extirpate these savages, in order to make room for cultivators of the earth, it seems not improbable that rum may be the appointed means. It has already annihilated the tribes who formerly in habited the sea coast" (*Autobiography*, p. 376).

Franklin's denunciation of "rum" was not dictated solely by humanitarian or moral considerations. In last analysis it was a political issue, since rum was imported from the West Indies. In the Preface to *Poor Richard Improved* for 1765, he undertook to convince his fellow countrymen that it was a patriotic duty "to supply ourselves from our own Produce at home":

> To this end, I have collected and written a few plain Instructions, which you will find in the Right Hand Pages of each Month; *First* for making good Wine of our own wild Grapes. *Secondly*, for raising Madeira Wine in those Provinces. *Thirdly* for the Improvement of our Corn Spirits, so as they may be preferable to rum.—And this seems very material, for as we raise more Corn than the *English West-India* Islands can take off, and since we cannot now well sell it to the foreign Islands, what can we do with the Overplus better, than to turn it into Spirit, and thereby lessen the Demand for *West-India* Rum, which our Grain will not pay for? *Fourthly* for supplying ourselves with a Syrup, every way superior to Molasses; and *Fifthly* for obtaining Sugar from our own Vegetables, in reasonable Plenty.

On the pages indicated by Franklin are found elaborations of the five points listed above. As a substitute for cane sugar, he suggested sugar and syrup to be obtained from beets, honey, apples and maple. He also gave directions "How to manage the Distiling a Spirit from Rye, or other Grains that shall be preferable to common Rum," for which the reader is referred to the original text of the *Almanach*, as the present editor has not been able to submit it to the judgment of experts. Finally he condemned, in terms to be remembered by social historians, the home product, as "The Corn Spirits made in our Country, have generally a vile burnt Smell and Taste that renders them very disagreeable." From which we may assume that Franklin was not so much opposed to whiskey as to bad corn liquor.

Although he was still in England during the whole year 1768, the *Almanach* for 1769 contains much material bearing his mark. It deserves further study and unfortunately is too abundant to be reproduced here. Two items, however, deal so manifestly with the preoccupations he had at the time that they must be reprinted as a fit conclusion to the considerations given above.

The first one is a short essay on temperance clearly reflecting the views of Tryon:

> CONTENTMENT, and COVETOUSNESS, TEMPERANCE and GLUTTONY, SOBRIETY and DRUNKEDNESS, compared, showing their respective Effects on our Happiness and Misery.
>
> Content will give a Relish to all my Pleasure, and make me epicurise upon my little Fortune, and enjoy to the full Height all that I have; whilst Covetousness would let me starve in the midst of Plenty, and make a Beggar of me, though I wallowed in Gold.
>
> Temperance and Sobriety will give me Life and Health, a calm and free Exercise of my Reason;

whilst Gluttony and Drunkedness will enervate my Body, and stupefy my Soul, make me live like a beast, and die like a Fool. For Pleasure has a bewitching Faculty, the more we taste it, the more we hanker after it; and therefore the best Way to avoid being captivated by that Syren, is to stop our Ears to her Charms; when we have often balked our Appetites, by denying them what they crave, they will in a while grow so quiet, that they will crave no more.

The second piece of advice might have been directed to Deborah as well as to Franklin himself. His very limited budget did not permit him to entertain as generously as he used to do and, even in his absence, it seems that his friends had kept up the pleasant custom to meet at his house. Already in the *Almanach* for 1745 he had noted that: "Fools make Feasts and Wise Men eat them." He repeated the advice in a letter to his wife and it is not unlikely that the following item expresses at least his budgetary intentions:

"Let not thy Table exceed the fourth Part of thy Income; see thy Provision be solid, and not far fetched, fuller of Substance than of Art; be wisely frugal in thy Preparation, and freely chearful in thy entertainment."

HOME COOKING AND DEBORAH

If we are to believe the *Autobiography*, Franklin kept up at least some of his frugal ways after he married: "My breakfast was a long time bread and milk (no tea) and I ate it out of a two penny porringer with a pewter spoon." But Deborah was an excellent cook and we can only guess how long her husband was able to resist the appetizing temptations she placed before him. Because of his official position, he also considered it his duty to keep an open house and a table generously appointed. It was not solely a matter of duty. When he was away from home, he hankered after the unexcelled productions of his own kitchen and Deborah took every care to keep him well supplied with choice dishes, which he generously shared with his companions. Unfortunately Franklin's correspondence with his wife has not yet been published in full. A few characteristic quotations might suffice pending a more complete survey of the existing letters.

On January 25, 1756, Franklin wrote to Deborah from Gnadenhutten:

"We have enjoyed your roast beef; and this day began on the roast veal. All agree that they are both the best that ever were of the kind. Your citizens that have their dinners hot and hot, know nothing of good eating. We find it in much better perfection when the kitchen is four score miles from the dining room.

"The apples are extremely welcome, and do bravely to eat after our salt pork; the minced pies are not yet come to hand, but I suppose we shall find them among the things expected up from Bethlehem on Tuesday; the capillaire is excellent but none of us having taken cold as yet, we have only tasted it" (Smyth, III, 324).

When he sailed for England at the end of 1764, he left unfinished in Philadelphia the house he had long "set his Heart upon" and which he intended to furnish and decorate to his taste. He sent to Deborah elaborate instructions about the "blue room" and the furniture (see Edward M. Riley, Franklin's Home, in *Historic Philadelphia* Transactions of the A.P.S. 43, part 1). But one of the most important features of the new dwelling was to be the kitchen for which Franklin had invented many "contrivances" though his good wife would probably not know how either to set up or to manipulate them. What a pity the letter giving "written directions" on how to set the oven has not been found! One may be certain that Franklin had given full flight to his inventive genius, for there is no doubt that he was an inventor in these homely matters as well as in fields considered more worthy of scientific attention. He politely pretended to be very glad that in his absence his friends had honored the new dining room with their company, but he was peeved that nobody had written "how the Kitchen Chimneys perform" (July 13, 1766. Smyth, IV, 391).

Amusingly enough one of the first letters to the press concerning the Stamp Act deals with gastronomy. An anonymous writer had declared in the *Gazetteer* that, "the Americans, should they resolve to drink no more tea, can by no means keep that Resolution, their Indian corn not affording an agreeable or easy digestible breakfast." Franklin was hurt to the quick and in his indignation became almost lyrical.

His answer deserves to be reprinted in full in all the treatises dealing with American cooking, and widely distributed for the edification and confusion of ignorant foreigners who sniff at good American dishes. Here it will be quoted only in part:

> Pray let me, an American, inform the gentleman, who seems ignorant of the matter, that Indian corn, take it for all in all, is one of the most agreeable and wholesome grains in the world; that its green leaves roasted are a delicacy beyond expression; that samp, hominy, succatash, and nokehock, made of it, are so many pleasing varieties; and that johny or hoecake, hot from the fire, is better than a Yorkshire muffin—But if Indian corn were so disagreeable and indigestible as the Stamp Act, does he imagine we can get nothing else for breakfast?—Did he never hear that we have oatmeal in plenty, for water gruel or burgoo; as good wheat, rye and barley as the world affords, to make frumenty; or toast and ale; that there is every where plenty of milk, butter and cheese; that rice is one of our staple commodities; that for tea, we have sage and bawm in our gardens, the young leaves of the sweet hickery or walnut, and above all, the buds of our pine, infinitely preferable to any tea from the Indies; while the islands yield us plenty of coffee and chocolate?—Let the gentleman do us the honour of a visit in America, and I will engage to breakfast him every day in the month with a fresh variety, without offering him either tea or Indian corn (January 2, 1766. Smyth, IV, 395).

This was not simply propaganda. For obvious reasons, Franklin felt that he had to economize. He worried about the expenses which Deborah could not avoid in order to entertain "the great many visitors" who had long been "in the Practice and habit" of inviting themselves to his house. He added significantly: "For my own Part I live here as frugally as possible, not to be destitute of the Comforts of Life, making no Dinners for anybody, and contenting myself with a single Dish when I dine at home" (June 20, 1767. Smyth, IV, 395). Should one recall that this Spartan austerity was far less rigorous in practice than Franklin admitted and that he very seldom dined at home. The fact remains, however, that even if he particularly enjoyed "nice things," like "Floating Islands" and what not, when invited by one of his many English friends (Smyth, V, 338), he missed the simple and wholesome fare of America. Thanks to Deborah, he was provided with an abundant supply of American products. "The Nocake is very good and I thank you for it," wrote he to his wife, August 5, 1767, and we may well suppose that he cooked it for breakfast. Six months later he had received another consignment of food: "I have received also the Indian and buckwheat meal, that they brought from you, with the apples, cranberries and nuts, for all which I thank you. They all proved good, and the apples were particularly welcome to me and my friends, as there happens to be scarce of any kind in England this year. We are much obliged to the captains, who are so good as to bring these things for us, without charging anything for their trouble" (Smyth, V, 96).

Some of the nuts were offered to a "certain great Lady, the best woman in England," who was "graciously pleased to accept them and to say that they were excellent." On several occasions he expressed real anxiety fearing that the apples would spoil because the ship was delayed. At the beginning of 1772, after receiving a particularly generous consignment, he waxed quite sentimental:

"The buckwheat and Indian meal are come safe and good. They will be a great refreshment to me this winter; for since I cannot be in America, everything that comes from thence comforts me a little, as being something like home. The dried peaches, too, are excellent, those dried without their skins. The parcel in their skins are not so good. The apples are the best I ever had, and came with the least damage. The sturgeon you mention did not come, but that is not so material" (Bigelow, V, 207).

Early in December of the same year, Deborah sent him a barrel of apples with another of cranberries, which came in good order, "all sound" (December 1, 1772, Bigelow, V, 207). At the beginning of the following year he had not yet received the usual shipment, but Captain Allen, in order to relieve his distress, gave him a barrel of excellent apples. Soon he was plentifully supplied, for Deborah had probably alerted several good friends. In February he could acknowledge not only the apples sent by his "dear child," but two barrels sent from New York by Bache, one from Captain Winn and one from Captain Falconer (Smyth, VI, 7).

Despite the assertion, already noted, that owing to his early education he scarcely noticed the quality of food when traveling, he was particularly concerned with his comfort on shipboard. At a date which cannot be determined exactly he wrote a significant essay on the subject. It has been published by Sparks under the title of "Precautions to be used by those who are about to undertake a sea voyage" (Sparks, II, 106). He elaborated upon it in the *Maritime Observations*, written for David Le Roy, at sea, on board the *London Packet*, August 1785. Only a few quotations from the earlier version will be given here.

Franklin advised the prospective traveler not to trust any sea captain in the matter of food, but to take along ample supplies of "good tea, ground coffee, chocolate, wine of that sort you like best, cider, dried raisins, almonds, sugar, capillaire, citrons, rum, eggs dipped in oil, portable soup, bread twice baked etc." He proclaimed that "The most disagreeable thing at sea is the cookery" and on the occasion recalled a saying he had already used in his *Almanach*: "Hence comes the proverb used among the English sailors, that God sends meat, and the Devil cooks." Therefore it was recommended to provide oneself with quite an equipment:

"You may yourself with a lamp and a boiler, by the help of a little spirit, prepare some food, such as soup, hash &c. A small oven made of tin plate is not a bad piece of furniture; your servant may roast in it a piece of mutton or pork. If you are tempted to eat salt beef, which is often very good, you will find that cider is the best liquor to quench the thirst generally caused by salt meat or salt fish. Sea biscuit, which is too hard for the teeth of some people may be softened by steeping it, but bread double baked is the best . . ."

For the rest, the reader is requested to refer to the complete text of the "Observations," but one recipe at least deserves a special mention:

"Pease often boil badly, and do not become soft; in

such case by putting a two-pound shot into the kettle, the rolling of the vessel, by means of this bullet, will convert the pease into a kind of porridge, like mustard."

Whether Franklin or some unknown ship cook should receive credit for the invention has not been ascertained. What is probably more important for the historian to remember is the sincere attachment of the Sage of Philadelphia for his home and his home country, a sentiment which manifested itself in such a prosaic matter as his daily diet. In this respect he had not been spoiled by his long stay in England. It remains now to see whether Paris succeeded in denationalizing Franklin's native taste.

PARIS

During the eighteenth century, the "philosophical spirit" invaded all the fields of human activity. It heralded a complete revolution in the art of eating and cooking. The gustatory and olfactory sensations, stigmatized by theologians, such as Bossuet, as low and impure, were rehabilitated. Two famous Jesuits, P. P. Brumoy and Bougeant did not think it unworthy of their calling to contribute a scholarly introduction to the *Dons de Comus* by the well known cook François Marin. Meusnier de Querlon, who corresponded with Franklin, wrote for the edition of 1750 a preface in which the influence of Tryon and Cheyne is manifest and the comparison between cooking and the arts emphasized. To please the ladies musically inclined, François Lebas, the "bon cuisinier," published *Le*

Festin Joyeux ou la Cuisine mise en musique, Paris, 1738. The preparation of food was rationalized in *La Cuisinière bourgeoise* of Menon, Paris 1746, the success of which lasted for more than a century. It is still considered a real classic. Diet had always been part of medicine, but the food question became the concern of the economists, the physicists and the chemists.

In a large measure some of the changes which took place during the century can be attributed to the part played by the ladies in the society of the time. The main attraction of the dinners in which they participated or gave was not food but conversation. The dinners of Baron d'Holbach were heavy and substantial. Madame Helvétius preserved some of the tradition established by her husband when he was generously feeding several famished "hommes de lettres," but no less famous were the suppers of Madame Geoffrin where the simple fare consisted of "un poulet, des épinards et une omelette." To the enormous meals of the Age of Louis XIV had succeeded light "soupers," scientifically prepared and artistically served, for the French had discovered as well as Benjamin Franklin that "The Muses starve in a Cook's Shop." Yet even "philosophes" must get some nourishment. Hence the fashion for extracts, essences and concentrated substances. It was carried to such a degree that in his *Giphantie*, published in 1761, Tiphaine de la Roche predicted that the day would come when a few particles of different salts, dissolved in a glass of water, would provide at will "excellent Beaune, Nuits, Chambertin, etc." The same process would make available the instantaneous reconstruction of "all the fruits, the fishes, birds, fowls, game and meats." The ways of eating and cooking had undergone a transformation that justified Sébastien Mercier's declaration in his *Tableau de Paris*, "on ne sait manger que depuis un siècle."

To suggest that Benjamin Franklin scorned the refinements of the French tables would be an insult to his universal curiosity. But it must be admitted that he never evidenced the systematic interest displayed by Jefferson, who compiled a regular cook book giving long lists of French dishes and detailed recipes. Even when enjoying himself, apparently unreservedly, in the company of his French friends, he never forgot the cardinal principle of diplomacy inscribed in the treaties of 1778, "perfect reciprocity." He was willing to learn from them, but he was equally eager to introduce them to what was best in American or, to use the terminology of the time, in Anglo-American cooking. However much he loved the French he remained intensely American and could never be accused of being "Frenchified."

This constant ambivalence manifested itself in an amusing way when he went to Paris for the first time, in 1767. He fully enjoyed the gift he received on landing at Boulogne of "two doz. of excellent Bordeaux," for which he had no duty to pay. This pleasant experience did not prevent him from praising almost in the same terms the quality of the drinking water "which is purified by filtering it thro four cisterns filled with sand" (Smyth, V, 49).

When he returned to France in 1777, this time as an official envoy, he made it a point to repay in kind the generous hospitality tendered him by his French friends. One of his first cares was to engage a French cook and to fill his cellar. Some of the inventories of his liquid provisions have been preserved. In May

1777, he listed 50 bottles of "Champaigne." In February 1778, he had no less than 1,040 bottles of various wines of which we have the detail, including 209 bottles of "vin ordinaire" and 159 bottles of "Vin rouge de Bordeaux," bottled at Passy. On September 1, 1782, he had 1203 bottles in stock (Bigelow, VIII, 350 and Smyth, X, 316).

This ample supply was not used only for official entertainments. We also know that the cook had to prepare regularly for the five persons in Franklin's household a "déjeuner" consisting of bread and butter, honey, coffee, or chocolate with sugar" and a dinner with "a joint of beef, veal or mutton, fowl or game, deux entremets, un plat de patisseries, une assiette de fromage, biscuits, bonbons, glaces, 2 fois par semaine en été et une fois en hiver."

At the top of his social and diplomatic activity he dined "abroad" six days out of seven and, on Sundays, served dinner at home "with such Americans as pass this way." This was a far cry from Tryon's diet.

As a contrast to the theoretical *Way to Health*, one may compare the clinical observations Franklin made of his physical condition consigned in a memorandum published by E. Hale, *Franklin in France*, Boston, 1887. Vol. 1, p. 247. It is dated Passy, Oct. 4, 1778. He had noted that his constitution had undergone alarming changes "within the last 3 or 4 years," and he undertook to study them systematically, "in order to ascertain what are hurtful or beneficial." Already in 1773, Sir John Pringle had advised him to abstain from "salted meat and cheese." He took due note of the prescription and confessed shamelessly, "which advice I did not much follow, often forgetting it."

Three entries in the Memorandum of 1778 illustrate

his hesitation and perplexity as well as a very human weakness:

"October 1, I ate a hearty supper, much cheese and drank a good deal of champagne. The 3rd I ate no breakfast, but a hearty dinner, and at night found my back itch extremely near the shoulders, which continues to-day the 4th. I ate some salted beef at dinner yesterday, but no much..."

"October 6, Drink but one glass of wine to-day... I begin to think it will be better for me to abstain from wine. My dinner to-day was mutton boiled, and fowl, with a good deal of fruit."

"Oct. 12. I have lately drank but little wine..." Then there is the humble admission, in his dialogue with Madame la Goute, that he was eating "inordinate breakfast, four dishes of tea, with cream, and one or two buttered toasts, with slices of hung beef, which I fancy are not the things most easily digested." He was too good an observer not to realize that such a diet was detrimental to his health and he made a full confession of his sins in the famous *Dialogue*. His consolation was that by warning him sharply when he departed too widely from a temperant regimen, Gout had saved him "from the palsy, dropsy and apoplexy, one or the other" would have done for him long ago but for these timely reminders. Such apparently was the generally accepted medical opinion. It had just been reiterated in a thesis defended before the Ecole de Médecine, on January 9, 1766, in a thesis that Franklin may have known: *An arthritis naturcæ beneficium?*

The American plenipotentiary had also another excuse. He thoroughly enjoyed dining "abroad," but many of these dinners were in part a matter of duty. They provided an opportunity to meet informally important people, officials of the royal government, influential writers and to prepare the ground for serious business.

We are particularly well informed on the dinners given by abbé Morellet on the first Sunday of each month. Full accounts of these memorable meetings have been preserved in the *Mémoires historiques sur le XVIIIe siècle*, by Dominique-Joseph Garat (Vol. I, 555-559) and by abbé Morellet himself, in his *Mémoires* (Chap. XV, 295-321). On these occasions the servants were kept away, for Morellet did not trust anybody in the preparation of these gastronomical experiments. New recipes were devised, new cooking utensils were invented and tested and the abbé "called upon all the genius displayed in this domain by the British and Anglo-Americans." The fare was delicious but never superabundant: "it was not enough for a dish to be good; it had to be superior." At irregular intervals during the meal, were circulated small glasses containing "delightful aromas blended with exquisite care" so as to prevent the stock of ideas from getting exhausted. At this point, Garat added significantly: "One knows what a great inventor Franklin was in this domain, as great in fact as when he was snatching the thunder from heaven and the scepter from tyrants!" What more could be said except that the patient reader will find in this booklet the recipe for one of these stimulating mixtures, very likely due to the inventive genius of Dr. Franklin?

These reunions were very gay, wrote abbé Morellet; they were graced by the presence of pretty and talented ladies. The later part of the evening was usually devoted to musical entertainments given by the most famous artists of the time. On a memorable occasion, the heavenly tunes of the harmonica were heard; at other times the guests sang some drinking songs composed especially for the evening and alluding to contemporary events. Such was the song written by Morellet in honor of "notre Benjamin." Franklin himself contributed "une petite chanson à boire" which he had written some fifty years earlier and probably the bagatelle giving a fanciful etymology of "deviner" and "divin."

Whether he participated actively in the discussions is another matter. He admitted in the *Ephémères* that he always had some difficulty in following a conversation in which four or five Frenchmen were engaged, "all talking at the same time." He probably preferred the more intimate dinners recalled by abbé de la Roche, when "two or three good friends" sat at a good table to discuss "morals, politics and philosophy." Such were the conditions found at the house of Madame Helvétius. There Franklin could meet all the literati and philosophers of the time and freely express himself since several of the guests could speak English quite well. There he met regularly and frequently abbé de la Roche, abbé Arnaud, Marmontel, abbé Morellet and a young medical student, Cabanis, then in his early twenties who was treated by Madame Helvétius as an adopted son.

What Franklin learned from him can only be guessed, but even a superficial study of the great work of Cabanis, *Rapports du Physique et du Moral de l'Homme*. Paris, 1805, would bring out convincing evidence that the young physician profited much from Franklin's conversation. The preface of the book, the chapter on "L'influence du régime sur les habitudes morales," remind one of many of the maxims printed in the *Almanachs* and of the "Rules to find out a fit measure of meat and drink." The chapter "Du sommeil," in which Franklin is specifically quoted, shows the definite influence of the *Art of Procuring Pleasant Dreams*. Even the maxim that sums up the chapters on nutrition, "L'estomac gouverne la cervelle," could have been written by the Sage of Passy and Philadelphia.

It would not be paradoxical to suggest that further research would demonstrate a limited but definite influence of Franklin on Brillat Savarin's famous *Physiologie du goût*. The author had spent several years in America during the French Revolution and he certainly was familiar with Franklin's writings. Meditation XX, on "The influence of diet on rest, sleep and dreams" contains the same prescriptions and comes to the same conclusions as Franklin's essay on the *Art of Procuring Pleasant Dreams*. The formula in which Brillat Savarin listed the conditions for enjoying a good meal, "at least acceptable fare, good wine, pleasant companions, and after dinner some entertainment," could have been written by Franklin. It expresses roughly the epicurean side of his gastronomic philosophy.

SCIENTIFIC EXPERIMENTS

According to a legend hard to uproot, the "philosophes" were men fond of systems and more interested in theoretical constructions than in practical applications. This is certainly untrue of the Economists and

Physiocrats. Back of their theories was an intense and earnest desire to secure for the peoples of Europe and even of the world what, in our modern parlance, might be termed "freedom from hunger." To procure enough food to survive was one of the main preoccupations of the American pioneers. In Europe where famines were frequent and the people were at the mercy of a bad crop, the need was even more vital.

In France the problem was summed up in the cry of the famished multitude "give us bread" tragically repeated from the Lord's prayer. For countless ages the making of bread had been left to empirical practices. Just at the time when Franklin arrived in France, a group of "philosophes" including chemists, physicists and physicians had decided to study methodically the art of the baker. The story of the experiment could be reconstructed from the *Mémoires secrets de la République des lettres*, the *Journal de Paris* and a large still unpublished correspondence in the Franklin papers. It is hoped that sometime it will be written in full.

As early as November 1778, Franklin attended a "grand repas expérimental" given by M. d'Espagnac to taste the potato bread made by "le sieur Parmentier apothicaire des Invalides." This marked the opening of the first scientific school of bakery. From that time on Franklin kept in touch with the various experiments carried out to discover a proper substitute for wheat flour. His most important contribution was to attempt to make the French accept the use of Indian corn or maize in the making of different sorts of breads.

First, he obtained from America corn meal and corn flour which he sent to Cadet de Vaux, and even as shown in a letter recently discovered by Professor

A. O. Aldridge, samples of bread manufactured under his direction (*Franklin and his French Contemporaries*, p. 176. New York, 1957). Then he added "je vous envoye la Recette pour le faire. Si vous jugez à propos d'en faire l'Essaye à l'Ecole de Boulangerie" (Feb. 4, 1784). The recipe has not been found, but there is every reason to believe that it was the origin of the paper giving instructions to mix wheat flour and corn flour, probably in Cadet de Vaux's hand, preserved in the papers of the Society and reproduced in this publication.

On April 28, 1785, Franklin sent to Cadet de Vaux a dissertation on the use of Maize. It was translated and published in the *Journal de Paris*, April 17, 1785. A press copy of the original in English has been preserved in the collections of the Library of Congress.

The experiments were so successful that Franklin decided to take with him several of the productions of the French "patisseur" on his way back to America.

As was often the case with him as well as with many of his contemporaries Franklin was impelled in this circumstance by various considerations. His motives were scientific and humanitarian; they were also patriotic, for America already produced a large surplus of corn, the exportation of which would have helped to repay in part the debt to the Royal government.

More picturesque was his invention of the *electric jack*. In one of his memoirs on electricity he had playfully described a dinner he intended to give on the banks of the Schuylkill:

"A turkey is to be killed for dinner by the *electrical shock*, and roasted by the *electrical jack*, before a fire kindled by the *electrified bottle*: then the healths of all the famous electricians in *England, Holland, France,* and *Germany* are to be drank in *electrified bumpers* under the discharge of guns from *the electrical battery*" (April 29, 1749. Smyth, II, 410).

The description of the *electrical jack* which might puzzle the reader is found in a letter to Collinson (Experiment 21, Smyth, II, 21, 23).

Almost twenty-five years later, when Dalibard was translating this letter, it came to the mind of the Frenchman that it would be desirable to present this scientific experiment "habillé à la française," for the benefit of that "frivolous nation," and to examine whether the flesh of an animal killed by electricity would not be tenderized in such a way that it could be eaten at once? (*Oeuvres de M. Franklin*, Paris, 1773. I, 332).

He requested from Franklin a supplement of information and Franklin obliged with a long letter of which only the French translation has been preserved. He refused to commit himself, reporting only that "persons who have eaten fowls killed by our drole de petit tonnerre and dressed immediately, have asserted that the flesh was remarkably tender." He also gave detailed instructions for the operator "lest he should happen to make the experiment on his own flesh, instead of that of the fowl" (Smyth, I, 332-334). The warning is still valid and should be kept in mind by anyone tempted to verify Dr. Dubourg's hypothesis.

THE RECIPES

THE collection of recipes in the Franklin papers consists of (1) 16 pages in French probably not arranged in the original order. One leaf bears the inscription "Rec^ts. translated into French" although the pages following it are in English. (2) separate recipes a) for Orange shrub in English; b) Method for making Spruce Beer, title in English and text in French; c) Method for making Raisin wine, in English endorsed "From Mr. Viney." It is an unsystematic collection. The texts are written in different hands by persons whose French was fairly good but spelling uncertain. One recipe exists in two versions, the first one a draft much written over, the second one a fair copy.

An attempt has been made to translate back into English the recipes given in French and as far as could be ascertained to reconstitute the style of the original From the beginning it appeared that Franklin had not invented all the recipes however extended may have been his proficiency in the culinary art. At this point arose difficulties to be expected in work of that kind. Makers of cookbooks from the most ancient times have always borrowed freely from their predecessors. English cookbooks of the eighteenth century are no exception to that rule; to make it more puzzling their authors also made a free use of the French books on the subject. In a sense, Franklin was bringing coal to Newcastle and was rendering unto the French what rightly belonged to them.

The present editor did not feel qualified to trace the history of every recipe and to achieve a scholarly and critical edition. At a time it was thought and hoped that Franklin had chiefly used *The Frugal Housewife, or Complete Woman Cook* by Susannah Carter of Clerkenwell, London. Printed for F. Newberry at the Corner of St. Paul's Church-Yard. Boston, reprinted and sold by Edes and Gill, in Queenstreet. Circa 1772, with engravings by Paul Revere. He may have taken two or three recipes from it. A more extensive study led to believe that the book probably used was *The English Housewifery. Exemplified in above Four Hundred and Fifty Receipts* by Elizabeth Moxon, Leeds, n.d. the fifth edition of which came out around 1780. It is to be noted, however, that the French texts were not mere translations; they present in most instances delicate improvements and refinements due either to the translator or to some culinary artist who experimented with the recipes.

Our search came to an end with the finding of Mrs. Hannah Glasse's great book, *The Art of Cookery, Made plain and easy ... By a Lady*, of which a new and more complete edition was published anonymously in London, around 1760. Obviously it was Franklin's *vade mecum* when he was in France and the main source of his gastronomic inspiration.

A curious case is that of the "oyster sauce" which seems to have entirely disappeared from French cookbooks but has survived in a modified form in some parts of America. Although all the French handbooks of the eighteenth century give a formula for it the recipe in our collection has no equal anywhere.

Four recipes belong undoubtedly in the Anglo-American field.

The first and most important one is the recipe for "Tranches de bœuf grillées." "Bifteck" has become such a regular item of the French menus that it seems paradoxical to imagine that the French did not always enjoy it. Such is the case, however. Before the end of the eighteenth century they always served beef with very complicated sauces. *L'Almanach des Gourmands* for 1803, speaking of English cookery, notes that "beef steak is the main course of their dinner. It is something that fully deserves that one should cross the Channel to get acquainted with it. With us it is only a hors d'œuvre; yet when properly prepared very few dishes can compare with it."

"Orange shrub" is found in many English cook books but nowhere with the same exact formula and scientific directions which seem to have been written by a scientist trained in laboratory methods.

We would like to fancy that the recipe for the mince pie was frequently used by Deborah. When tried by the editor and his associates it was declared far superior to any we had ever tasted.

The "White caudle" has no place in the dining room though Madame la Goute would have approved of it; it cannot be recommended as a regular drink for a healthy man, even with the addition of white wine or lemon.

Two exotic recipes already printed in Franklin's works were added. One dealing with Chinese cooking and still available in any Chinese restaurant. The other one has become popular in recent years under the name of yogurt.

The recipes for the use of corn flour have already been discussed.

It is hoped that some venturesome souls imbued with true historical spirit will experiment with these recipes. On such occasions they will relive in imagination abbé Morellet's dinners when wit and philosophical conversations gave a unique flavor to these culinary preparations. They will do well also to remember the cardinal axiom of Franklin's friends "a very few courses, very little of everything, but everything excellent."

HOME AGAIN

Back in Philadelphia, comfortably settled in his house, Franklin often thought of his French friends, of the musical evenings, the long conversations, the pretty women who worshipped him, sat at his feet and sometimes on his lap. In letters he expressed a nostalgic longing certainly pleasant to his friends in Paris. Of that sentimental tenor is the letter he wrote in French to Madame Helvétius: "Philadelphia, ce 2 octobre, 1785... Hier soir etoit Mercredi. A dix heures de Matin j'ai pensé de vous, de votre Maison, de votre Table, de vos Amis etc. . . ." The condition of his health, the increasingly sharp warnings given by his ailments did not allow him much freedom in his diet. He wrote to Le Veillard, April 16, 1787: "I live temperately, drink no wine and use daily the exercise of the dumb bell." He drowned his melancholy regret not in wine, but if we are to believe him, in "les eaux epurées de Passy," which he was drinking with great satisfaction "as they kept well, and seem to be rendered more agreeable by the long voyage." In apparent contradiction to his professed austerity, he complained to Le Veillard "that the wine which had arrived was not well secured and bottled" (Oct. 24, 1788). But a letter of William Temple dealing with the same subject and repeating the same complaint permits to suppose that the "vin de Cahussac" was intended for the grandson and not for the grandfather.

As he remembered his friends he wished to be remembered by them and he could not think of any better way than to send them some of the choicest products of America. On March 20, 1786, he wrote to Ferdinand Grant a business letter ending in a more familiar style:

"I add a few lines to give you a little Trouble in requesting you to receive and divide among some of my Friends a few Hams (jambons) and some Cakes of our Soap. The Hams are in a Cask; and have Labels on them to denote who they are for; I send them because Strangers here admire them for their good Taste and the Sweetness of their Fat, which is all made by their Feeding on Maize, and I hope they will come good to hand."

The soap was no less remarkable as it was "thought to be the finest in the World for Shaving & for Washing Cinces and other things of delicate colours." The recipients of the cakes of soap included 18 persons and we may suppose that the admirable hams were to be distributed among them.

He had had much experience and made many experiments. He had grown old and physically feeble but he had remained the same. He loved his foreign friends and their hospitable lands but he loved America best. It was pleasant to remember the "nice" dinners of

Paris, Passy and Auteuil, but it does not take great perspicacity to feel that he preferred the home products, apples from York, the good sweet taste of the Pennsylvania hams, the mince pies that Deborah used to make, and even a slice of hung beef or a piece of the salted fish that his sister kept sending him from Boston. We can be certain that he enjoyed better than chocolate the substantial cakes made out of corn meal. Perhaps his taste had been educated, but as Poor Richard had said in 1748, he wanted "Food not costly vain, but plentifully good." Such food was produced in abundance by America and this was a source of legitimate pride. In lesser men such a pride takes easily the form of chauvinism. Under the conditions existing even now in many countries, it may not be out of place to recall that Franklin was probably the first American to propose, as early as 1771, *A Plan for Benefitting Distant Unprovided Countries* and "with all his heart, to subscribe to a voyage intended to communicate in general those benefits we enjoy, to countries destitute of them in the remote parts of the globe."

GILBERT CHINARD

The WAY To
HEALTH,
LONG
Life and Happiness:

Or, A Discourse of

TEMPERANCE,

And the Particular
Nature of all Things requisite for the Life of
Man; As, All sorts of *Meats, Drinks, Air, Exercise,* &c.
with special Directions how to use each of them to the
best Advantage of the BODY and MIND.

Shewing from the true ground of Nature, whence most
Diseases proceed, and how to prevent them.

To which is Added,

A Treatise of most sorts of ENGLISH HERBS,
With several other remarkable and most useful Observations, very necessary for all Families. The whole Treatise displaying the most hidden secrets of *Philosophy*, and made easie and familiar to the meanest Capacities, by various Examples and Demonstrances.

The like never before Published.

Communicated to the World for a general Good,
By *THOMAS TRYON*, Student
in PHYSICK.

The Second Edition, with Amendments.

LONDON:

Printed by *H.C.* for D. Newman, at the *King's-Arms* in the *Poultry*, 1691.

THE
ART of COOKERY,

MADE

PLAIN and EASY.

CHAP. I.
Of ROASTING, BOILING, &c.

THAT profeſſed cooks will find fault with touching upon a branch of cookery which they never thought worth their notice, is what I expect: however, this I know, it is the moſt neceſſary part of it; and few ſervants there are, that know how to roaſt and boil to perfection.

I do not pretend to teach profeſſed cooks, but my deſign is to inſtruct the ignorant and unlearned (which will likewiſe be of great uſe in all private families) and in ſo plain and full a manner, that the moſt illiterate and ignorant perſon, who can but read, will know how to do every thing in cookery well.

I ſhall firſt begin with roaſt and boiled of all ſorts, and muſt deſire the cook to order her fire according to what ſhe is to dreſs; if any thing very little or thin, then a pretty little briſk fire, that it may be done quick and nice; if a very large joint, then be ſure a good fire be laid to cake. Let it be clear at the bottom; and when your meat is half done, move the dripping-

B   pan

The Rules and Recipes

Rules of Health and Long Life, and to Preserve from Malignant Fevers, and Sickness in General

(POOR RICHARD FOR 1742)

Eat and drink such an exact Quantity as the Constitution of thy Body allows of, in reference to the Services of the Mind.

They that study much, ought not to eat so much as those that work hard, their Digestion being not so good.

The exact Quantity and Quality being found out, is to be kept to constantly.

Excess in all other Things whatever, as well as in Meat and Drink, is also to be avoided.

Youth, Age, and Sick require a different Quantity.

And so do those of contrary Complexions; for that which is too much for a flegmatick Man, is not sufficient for a Cholerick.

The Measure of Food ought to be (as much as possibly may be) exactly proportionate to the Quality and Condition of the Stomach, because the Stomach digests it.

That Quantity that is sufficient, the Stomach can perfectly concoct and digest, and it sufficeth the due Nourishment of the Body.

A greater Quantity of some things may be eaten than of others, some being of lighter Digestion than others.

The Difficulty lies, in finding out an exact Measure; but eat for Necessity, not Pleasure, for Lust knows not where Necessity ends.

Wouldst thou enjoy a long Life, a healthy Body, and a vigorous Mind, and be acquainted also with the wonderful works of God? labour in the first place to bring thy Appetite into Subjection to Reason.

Rules to Find out a Fit Measure of Meat and Drink

(POOR RICHARD FOR 1742)

If thou eatest so much as makes thee unfit for Study, or other Business, thou exceedest the due Measure.

If thou art dull and heavy after Meat, it's a sign thou hast exceeded the due Measure; for Meat and Drink ought to refresh the Body, and make it chearful, and not to dull and oppress it.

If thou findest these ill Symptoms, consider whether too much Meat, or too much Drink occasions it, or both, and abate by little and little, till thou findest the Inconveniency removed.

Keep out of the Sight of Feasts and Banquets as much as may be; for 't is more difficult to refrain from good Cheer, when it 's present, than from the Desire of it when it is away; the like you may observe in the Objects of all the other Senses.

If a Man casually exceeds, let him fast the next Meal, and all may be well again, provided it be not too often done; as if he exceed at Dinner, let him refrain a Supper, &c.

A temperate Diet frees from Diseases; such are seldom ill, but if they are surprised with Sickness, they bear it better, and recover sooner; for most Distempers have their Original from Repletion.

Use now and then a little Exercise a quarter of an Hour before Meals, as to swing a Weight, or swing your Arms about with a small Weight in each Hand; to leap, or the like, for that stirs the Muscles of the Breast.

A temperate Diet arms the Body against all external Accidents; so that they are not so easily hurt by Heat, Cold or Labour; if they at any time should be prejudiced, they are more easily cured, either of Wounds, dislocations or Bruises.

But when malignant Fevers are rife in the Country or City where thou dwelst, 't is adviseable to eat and drink more freely, by Way of Prevention; for those are Diseases that are not caused by Repletion, and seldom attack Full-feeders.

A sober Diet makes a Man die without Pain; it maintains the Senses in Vigour; it mitigates the Violence of the Passions and Affections.

It preserves the Memory, it helps the Understanding, it allays the Heat of Lust; it brings a Man to a Consideration of his latter End; it makes the Body a fit Tabernacle for the Lord to dwell in; which makes us happy in this World, and eternally happy in the World to come, through Jesus Christ our Lord and Saviour.

Pour fondre du Beurre.

En fondant du beurre, il faut être très soigneux.

Votre Poelon doit être bien étamé. Mettez y un Cuillerée d'eau froide, un peu de farine et votre beurre coupé en morceaux: Soyez très attentif à remuer le poelon *constamment du même côté*, de peur que le beurre ne tourne en huile; quand le tout est fondu, faites le bouillir et il deviendra uni et fin.

Pour griller des Tranches de beuf.

Il faut d'abord que votre feu soit clair, et vif; votre gril étant très net, mettez le sur le feu: prenez alors les tranches de boeuf qui doivent être prises de la fesse du boeuf et coupées épais d'environ un demi-pouce; saupoudrez les avec un peu de sel et de poivre et mettez les sur le gril. Ne tournez pas vos tranches jusqu'a ce qu'un côté soit fini d'être grillé; alors quand vous les tournerez de l'autre côté, il y aura bientôt sur la surface un riche jus, qu'il faut être très attentif de ne pas perdre. Vos Tranches étant assez grillées otez les soigneusement du gril pour ne pas repandre le jus. Mettez les sur un plat bien chaud, couverez [sic] les avec un autre et portez les sur la table.

La grande delicatesse de ce Ragoût est de l'avoir très chaud et très succulant.

On peut, (si on l'aime), couper finement dans le plat, avant d'y mettre les Tranches, une échalotte ou deux, ou bien un oignon fin.

To Melt Butter.

In melting of butter you must be very careful; let your saucepan be well tinned, take a spoonful of cold water, a little dust of flour, and your butter cut to pieces: be sure to keep shaking your pan one way, for fear it should oil; when it is all melted, let it boil, and it will be smooth and fine. A silver pan is best, if you have one. *The Art of Cookery*, p. 5.

To broil steaks.

First have a very clear brisk fire; let your gridiron be very clean; put it on the fire, and take a chaffing dish with a few hotcoals out of the fire. Put the dish on it which is to lay your steaks on, then take fine rump steaks about half an inch thick; put a little pepper and salt on them, lay them on the gridiron, and (if you like it) take a shalot or two, or a fine onion and cut it fine; put it into your dish. Don't turn your steaks till one side is done, then when you turn the other side there will soon be fine gravy lie on the top of the steak, which you must be careful not to lose. When the steaks are enough, take them carefully off into your dish, that none of the gravy be lost; then have ready a hot dish and cover, and carry them hot to table, with the cover on. *The Art of Cookery*, p. 7.

Sauce pour des Canards ou des Lapins bouillis.

Lorsque vos Canards ou vos Lapins sont bouillis, il faut verser dessus des Oignons bouillis, ce que vous ferez de la manière suivante: Prenez des Oignons, pelez les et faites les bouillir dans une grande Quantité d'Eau; changez votre Eau, et laissez les encore bouillir environ deux Heures; tirez les et jettez les dans une Passoire pour égoutter, alors hachez les sur une table, et mettez les dans un Poilon, saupoudrez les avec un peu de farine. ajoutez y un peu de Lait ou de Crême, avec un bon Morceau de Beurre, mettez les ainsi sur le feu, et retirez les lorsque le Beurre sera fondu.

Alors vous verserez le tout sur vos Lapins ou vos Canards bouillis.

Sauce d'huitres pour un Dindon Bouilli.

Prenez une Chopine d'huitres exprimez en la Liqueur que vous conserverez, mettez les dans l'eau froide, lavez les et netoyez les bien, mettez les dans une terrine avec votre Liqueur dans laquelle vous mettrez un tige de Muscade, avec un peu de beurre enveloppé de farine, et le quart d'un Citron; faites les bouillir, ensuite, mettez y une demie Chopine de Crême, et faites bouillir doucement, le tout ensemble, cela fait otez en le Citron, la Muscade, exprimez le Jus d'un Citron dans la Sauce, alors vous la servirez dans une Sauciere.

Sauce for boiled ducks or rabbits.

To boiled ducks or rabbits, you must pour boiled onions over them, which is done thus: take the onions, peel them, and boil them in a great deal of water; shift your water, then let them boil about two hours, take them up and throw them into a cullender to drain, then with a knife chop them on a board; put them into a sauce-pan, just shake a little flour over them, put in a little milk or cream, with a good piece of butter; set them over the fire, and when the butter is melted they are enough.... *The Art of Cookery*, p. 9.

Oyster Sauce for a Boiled Turkey.

Take one Pint of oysters draw out the Liquor which you will set apart, put them in cold water, wash and clean them well, put them in an earthen dish with the Liquor, in which you will put a shred of Nutmeg, with a little butter strewed with flour and a quarter of a Lemon; boil them, then, put in a half Pint of Cream and boil slowly, all together; this done take out the Lemon, the Nutmeg, squeeze the Juice of a Lemon in the Sauce, then serve it in a Sauceboat. *Editor.*

Pâte feuilletée.

Prenez deux Pintes de farine et une Livre de Beurre, pétrissez les ensemble très finement et reduisez les avec l'eau froide en une pâte claire assez ferme pour qu'on puisse la travailler: alors roulez la de l'épaisseur d'environ une piece de 6 Francs étendez dessus une couche de Beurre, jettez y un peu de farine. repliez la et roulez la une seconde fois, repliez la encore et roulez la sept ou huit fois; alors elle sera propre pour toutes les Espèces de Pâtés ou tourtes qui demandent une Pâte feuilletée.

Pour faire un Pudding de Riz cuit au Four.

Faites bouillir une Livre de Riz jusqu'a ce qu'il soit amoli, alors égoutez en toute l'eau, et sechez le plus que vous pourrez sans pourtant le presser. ensuite ajoutez un bon morceau de Beurre que vous remuerez, et sucrez le à votre goût. Vous ajouterez une petite muscade rapée, vous remuerez bien le tout ensemble, vous le verserez dans une Casserole enduite de Beurre et le ferez cuire ainsi. Vous pouvez ajouter quelques Raisins de Corinthe pour changer.

Puff-paste.

Take a quarter of a peck of flour, rub fine half a pound of butter, a little salt, make it up into a light paste with cold water, just stiff enough to work it well up; then roll it out, and stick pieces of butter all over, and strew a little flour; roll it up and roll it out again; and do so nine or ten times, till you have rolled in a pound and a half of butter. This crust is mostly used for all sorts of pies. *The Art of Cookery*, p. 145.

A rice-pudding baked.

Boil a pound of rice just till it is tender; then drain all the water from it as dry as you can, but don't squeeze it; then stir in a good piece of butter, and sweeten to your palate. Grate a small nutmeg in, stir it all well together, butter a pan, and pour it in and bake it. You may add a few currants for change. *The Art of Cookery*, p. 245.

[Pour rôtir un Cochon de Lait]

Avant de mettre le Cochon de Lait devant le feu, prenez un peu de Sauge hachée très menu, un morceau de beurre gros comme une noix et un peu de poivre et de Sel, mettez les dans le Cochon, et cousez le avec du gros fil. Saupoudrez le jusqu'a ce que les Yeux tombent, ou que la peau soit bien rissolée. Soyez très attentif à recevoir tout le Jus qui tombe du Cochon, en mettant dessous, aussitôt que vous voyez qu'il en tombe, des Jattes ou des Poélons, que vous placerez dans la Léchefritte.

Quand le Cochon est assez rôti faites un feu clair prenez un torchon propre et mettez dedans un Quartron de beurre et frottez le Cochon avec, jusqu'à ce que la peau soit parfaitement rissolée. Ensuite tirez le Cochon du feu, mettez le dans un plat, coupez la tête et coupez le cochon en deux avant de le tirer de la broche. alors coupez les Oreilles et mettez en une à châque bout du plat, coupez aussi la machoire de dessous et mettez en une partie de chaque côté. fondez un peu de beurre, prenez le jus que vous avez conservé et mettez le dans votre beurre et faites le bouillir versez le tout dans le plat avec la servelle de Cochon coupée par morceaux et mêlée avec la Sauge, et servéz le ainsi sur la table.

To roast a pig.

Spit your pig and lay it to the fire, which must be a very good one at each end, or hang a flat iron in the middle of the grate. Before you lay your pig down, take a little sage shred small, a piece of butter as big as a walnut, and a little peper and salt; put them into the pig and sew it up with coarse thread, then flour it all over very well, and keep flouring it till the eyes drop out, or you find the crackling hard. Be sure to save all the gravy that comes out of it, which you must do by setting basons or pans under the pig in the dripping-pan, as soon as you find the gravy begins to run. When the pig is enough, stir the fire up brisk; take a coarse cloth, with about a quarter of a pound of butter in it, and rub the pig all over till the crackling is quite crisp, and then take it up. Lay it in your dish, and with a sharp knife cut off the head, and then cut the pig in two, before you draw out the spit. Cut the ears off the head and lay at each end, and cut the under jaw in two and lay on each side: melt some good butter, take the gravy you saved and put into it, boil it, and pour into the dish with the brains bruised fine, and the sage mixed all together, and then send it to table. *The Art of Cookery*, p. 3.

Recette d'un Pâté haché.

Prenez trois Livres de Graisse de Mouton hachée très menu.

Deux Livres de Raisins de Chorinte, bien épluché, lavé, essuyé et seché auprès du Feu.

Prenez un demi cent de Rénettes écorcées sans Pépins et coupées très fin.

Une demi-Livre du plus beau Sucre râpé finement.

Le Quart d'une Once de Fleur de Muscade.

Un Quart d'Once de Clous de Girofle.

Deux grosses Muscades.

Le tout pilé très fin.

Mettez le tout ensemble dans une grande Casserole, et remuéz le dans une demie-Chopine d'eau de vie et une demie Chopine de Vin de Malaga. Ensuite vous le mettrez dans un Pot de Fayance.

Quand vous ferez votre Paté, Prenez un plat, couvrez le d'une Croute de Pâté, mettéz y une Légére Couche de votre Mélange, et puis une Couche de Citron très mince; ensuite une autre Couche de votre Mélange haché, et une Couche de Pelures d'Oranges très fine. Pardessus tout cela, un légere Couche du Melange, exprimez y le Jus d'une Orange ou d'un Citron. Méttez une Croute égale à celle du dessous et méttez votre Pâte au Four.

To make mince pies the best way.

Take three pounds of suet shred very fine, and chopped as small as possible, two pounds of raisins stoned, and chopped as fine as possible, two pounds of currants nicely picked, washed, rubbed, and dried at the fire, half a hundred of fine pippins; pared, cored, and chopped small, half a pound of fine sugar pounded fine, a quarter of an ounce of mace, a quarter of an ounce of cloves, two large nutmegs; all beat fine; put all together into a great pan, and mix it well together with half a pint of brandy, and half a pint of sack; put it down close in a stone-Pot, and it will keep good four months. When you make your Pies, take a little dish, something bigger than a soup-plate, lay a very thin crust all over it, lay a thin layer of meat, and then a thin layer of citron cut thin, over that a little meat, squeeze half the juice of a fine Seville orange or lemon, and pour in three spoonfuls of red wine; lay on your crust, and bake it nicely. *The Art of Cookery*, p. 142.

Pour faire un Pudding de Pommes.

Faites une bonne Pate feuilletée, roulez la de façon qu'elle ait un demi pouce d'épaisseur, pélez vos pommes et coupez les par morceaux en assez grande quantité pour remplir la Croûte, et renfermez les dedans, liez le tout dans un linge et faites le bouillir, pendant deux heures si c'est un petit pudding, et pendant trois ou quatre heures, s'il est plus grand. lorsqu'il est assez cuit mettez le dans votre plat, coupez un marceau de la croute de dessus, ajoutez y du beurre et du sucre autant à votre gout qu'il vous plaira, remettez ensuite le marceau de croute coupé et servez le chaud sur la table.

fa[i]tes le pudding de poire de la même maniere.

Vous pouvez faire ainsi un Pudding de prunes de damas ou de toute autre Espece de prunes, d'abricôts, de cerises ou de meures et ils seront très bons.

Maniere de faire de la Biere avec de l'Essence de Spruce.—

Pour une Barrique contenant 80 Bouteilles, prenez un Pot d'Essence et 13 Livres de Mélasse.—ou autant de Sucre Brut; mélez les bien ensemble dans 20 Pintes d'Eau chaude: Remuez, les jusqu'à ce qu'ils moussent, versez les après dans la Barrique que vous remplirez d'Eau: Ajoutez alors une Chopine de bonne Levure, remuez bien le tout, et laissez le reposer 2 ou 3 Jours pour fermenter, après quoi vous boucherez la Barrique, et dans peu de Jours, il sera propre à mettre en Bouteilles, qui devront être parfaitement bien bouchées. Laissez les 10 à 12 Jours dans une Cave fraîche, après quoi la Bierre sera bonne à boire.

To make an apple pudding.

Make a good puff-paste, roll it out half an inch thick, pare your apples, and core them, enough to fill the crust, and close it up, tie it in a cloth and boil it. If a small pudding, two hours: if a large one three or four hours. When it is enough turn it into your dish, cut a piece of the crust out of the top, butter and sugar it to your palate; lay on the crust again, and send it to table hot. A pear pudding make the same way. And thus you may make a damson pudding, or any sort of plums, apricots, cherries, or mulberries, and are very fine. *The Art of Cookery*, p. 220.

A Way of making Beer with Essence of Spruce.

For a Cask containing 80 Bottles, take one Pot of Essence and 13 Pounds of Molasses.—or the same amount of unrefined Loaf Sugar; mix them well together in 20 Pints of hot Water: Stir together until they make a Foam, then pour it into the Cask you will then fill with Water: add a Pint of good Yeast, stir it well together and let it stand 2 or 3 Days to ferment, after which close the Cask, and after a few days it will be ready to be put into Bottles, that must be tightly corked. Leave them 10 or 12 Days in a cool Cellar, after which the Beer will be good to drink. *Editor.*

Pour faire une boisson qu'on appelle en Anglois White Caudle.

Prenez deux Pintes d'eau, metés y quatre cuillenées de Gruau d'Avoine, une tige ou deux de fleur de Muscade, un morceau de peau de Citron, faites bouillir le tout en le remuant souvent. Qu'il bouille un quart d'heure en prenant garde qu'il ne bouille davantage. alors vous le passerez à travers un gros tamis. lorsque vous userez de cette boisson, adoucissez la à votre gout, ajoutez y de la muscade rapée, et autant de vin qu'il est necessaire, et si ce n'est pas pour un malade, pressez y le jus d'un citron.

To make White Caudle.

You must take two quarts of water, mix in four spoonfuls of oatmeal, a blade or two of mace, a piece of lemon-peel, let it boil, and keep stirring it often. Let it boil about a quarter of an hour, and take care it does not boil over; then strain it through a coarse sieve. When you use it, sweeten it to your palate, grate in a little nutmeg, and what wine is proper; and if not for a sick person, squeeze in the juice of a lemon. *The Art of Cookery*, p. 237.

Orange Shrub.

To a Gallon of Rum two Quarts of Orange Juice and two pound of Sugar—dissolve the Sugar in the Juice before you mix it with the Rum—put all together in a Cask & shake it well—let it stand 3- or 4- Weeks & it will be very fine & fit for Bottling—when you have Bottled off the fine pass the thick thro' a Philtring paper put into a Funnell—that not a drop may be lost.

To obtain the flavour of the Orange Peel paire a few Oranges & put it in Rum for twelve hours—& put that Rum into the Cask with the other—

For Punch thought better without the Peel.

A Rec. to make Raisins wine
*From Mr Viney whose Wine
was remarkably good*

Take Malaga, or Raisins of the Sun, or any other you prefer; The Quantity 3^{cwt} to a Hhd—Pick the Raisins from the gross Stalk & put them into a Mashing Tub with a Tap & Tap Ouse, to prevent the Raisins obstructing the drawing off—Put 20 Gallons of Water, on the Fruit the first time which will just cover the Raisins. After they have soak'd 3 or 4 Days stir them Night & Morning—There must be a Cover fitted to the Tub just to keep the Raisins under Water—The time the Liquor must stand upon the Raisins is uncertain. but in moderate weather 12 or 14 days. but if very cold longer. Draw off half the Liquor put on; Put it into a clean Hogsh.^{d} with a Tile over the Bung-hole— Put just as much Water as will cover the Raisins again; for now the Raisins will begin to break, & stir with more ease than at first; the second Liquor must not stand quite so long as the first; Draw it off, & put it to the former in the Hogsh.^{d}, which will make it half full; Then put a few more Pails of Water just to make the Raisins stir easy; This if rightly conducted will fill the Hogsh^d: but it must not stand more than 8 or 9 Days; though if the Raisins taste sweet it must stand longer—If not enough to fill the Hogsh^d thro on a few more Pails of Water upon the same Raisins—It must be prest off with a Weight. Hand skrew or Jack—for now a much greater Quantity will come than from the former Drawings—Let it stand 6 Weeks or 2 Months, then draw it off the gross Leas—To every 20 Gall^s of Liquor add 1 Quart of neat Brandy to prevent a second

Fermentation; which must be carefully attended to; as it is very apt to alter in blossoming & ripening Season—But should it ferment, after it is drawn off. notwithstanding the Brandy; draw it off again into an open Cover: & let it stand 12 Hours. Rinse the Hogsh^d clean: dip a Piece of Rag in Flower of Brimstone & barn within side the Hogsh^d—Put the wine in again & leave the Pig hole open to give it Vent; Six Months after draw it off; which if fine will be the last time—& when settled will be fit to draw—February the last Month to make it in England—as Hott Weather will turn it sauer—

Recette pour faire des Tablettes de Bouillon à la maniere Angloise.

Prenez deux Eclanches de Veau et deux de Boeuf, otez en le Gras et coupez ensuite la Viande par tranches ajoutez-y moitié du Maigre d'un fort Jambon. Prenez un Quarteron de Beurre, etendez le au fond d'un grand Pot dans lequel vous mettez la Viande et les Os avec quatre onces d'Anchois 2 onces de Maces & six racines de Celeri, ayant soin d'ôter le verd et de les laver très proprement, coupez les très menu et 3 grosses Carotes coupées également très menu; mettez le tout dans un Chaudron que vous couvrirez tres exactement, et mettez le sur un feu moderé, et lors que le jus commence à se separer, enlevez le, jusqu'à ce qu'il soit tiré en totalité du Pot. Versez y ensuite assez d'eau pour que la Viande soit couverte et laissez le bouillir doucement en écumant la Graisse à mesure qu'elle s'eleve, jusqu'à ce que le bouillon paroisse épais comme de la Glace. Il faut prendre bien garde lors qu'il sera près d'être fait, de le laisser bruler. Mettez du Poivre de Cayenne à votre Gout, et versez ensuite dans des Plats de Terre trois lignes d'Epaisseur et laissez le ainsi jusqu'au jour suivant ou vous le couperez avec un Emporte Piéce rond de ferblanc, un peu plus grand qu'une Piece de six Francs. laissez ces petits Gateaux sur des Plats entre des Flanelles propres et mettez les au Soleil pour secher. Il vaut mieux faire ce Bouillon dans un Temps de Gelée. lorsqu'ils seront secs mettez les dans une boite de Fer blanc; ayant soin de mettre une Feuille de Papier entre chaque Rang et conservez les dans un Endroit sec.

Une Pinte d'eau bouillante versée sur une de ces Tablettes, ou Gateaux avec un peu de sel suffit pour

Recipe to make Bouillon Tablets in the English manner.

Take two Shoulders of Veal and two of Beef, cut off the Fat then slice the Meat add to it half the Lean of a large Ham. Take a quarter pound of Butter, spread it down the bottom of a large Pot into which you place the Meat and Bones, together with four ounces of Anchovies two ounces of Mace & six Celery roots, taking care to cut off the green part and wash them very thoroughly, shred them very small and 3 large Carrots also shredded very small; Put the whole into a large boiler which should be tightly covered, and set on a moderate fire, and when the juice begins to ooze out of the Meat dip it out of the Pot until it be entirely drawn. Then pour in enough water to cover the Meat and let it simmer while you skim the Fat as it comes on top until the bouillon looks as thick as glaze. Great care should be taken that it does not burn when it is nearly done. Add Cayenne Pepper as you please, then pour it into earthen dishes three lines thick and let it remain until the following day when you will cut it with a round Tin Punch, a little larger than a six francs Piece. Leave these small Cakes on dishes in between clean pieces of Flannel and set them in the Sun to dry. It is most proper to make this Bouillon in freezing weather. When they are dry put them in a Tin box; taking care to lay a Piece of Paper between each Row and keep in a dry Place.

One Pint of boiling water poured on one of these Tablets, or Cakes with a little salt is enough to obtain an excellent Bouillon. The longer they are kept, the better they are.

faire un excellent Bouillon. plus ils sont gardés et meilleurs ils sont.

Souvenez vous de tourner les Gateaux sur la Flanelle à mesure qu'ils sechent.

Ils font aussi un tres bon Jus ou Sauce aux Dindons et Volailles.

Remember to turn over the Cakes on the Flannel as they dry.

They also make a very good Gravy or Sauce for Turkeys and Fowls. *Editor.*

Mayz

It is remark'd in North America, that the English Farmers when they first arrive there, finding a Soil and Climate proper for the Husbandry they have been accustomed to, and particularly suitable for raising Wheat, they despise & neglect the Culture of Mayz: But observing the Advantage it affords to their Neighbours, the older Inhabitants, they by degrees get more and more into the Practice of Raising it; and the Face of the Country shows from time to time, that the Culture of that Grain goes on visibly augmenting.

The Inducements are, the many different Ways in which it may be prepared, so as to afford a wholesome and pleasing Nourishment to Men and other Animals.

1. The Family can begin to make use of it before the

time of full Harvest; for the tender green Ears stript of their Leaves and roasted by a quick Fire till the Grain is brown, and eaten with a little Salt or Butter, are a Delicacy. 2. When the Grain is riper and harder the Ears boil'd in their Leaves, and eaten with Butter are also good & agreable Food. The green tender Grains, dried [*can*] may be kept all the Year; and mixed with green Haricots also dried, make at any time a pleasing Dish, being first soak'd some hours in Water, and then boil'd. When the Grain is ripe and hard, there are also several Ways of using it. One is to soak it all Night in a Lessive, and then pound it in a large wooden Mortar with a wooden Pestle; the Skin of each Grain is by this means stript off, and the farinaceous part left whole, which being boil'd swells out into a white soft Pulp, and eaten with Milk, or with Butter and Sugar, is delicious. The dry Grain is also sometimes ground loosely, so as to be broke into Pieces of the size of Rice, and being winnow'd to separate the Bran, it is then boiled and eaten with Turkies or other Fowls as Rice.—Ground into a finer Meal, they make of it by Boiling a Hasty-pudding, or Bouillie, to be eaten with Milk, or with Butter and Sugar; this resembles what the Italians call Polenta. They make of the same Meal with Water and Salt, a hasty Cake which, being stuck against a Hoe or any flat Iron, is plac'd erect before the Fire, and so baked, to be used as Bread. Broth is also agreably thicken'd with the same Meal. They also parch it in this manner. An Iron Pot is fill'd with Sand, and set on the Fire till the Sand is very hot. Two or three Pounds of the Grain are then thrown in and well mix'd with the Sand by stirring. Each Grain bursts and throws out a white substance of twice its bigness. The Sand is separated by a Wire Sieve, and return'd into the Pot, to be again heated and repeat the Operation with fresh grain. That which is parch'd is pounded to a Powder in Mortars. This being sifted will keep long fit for Use. An Indian will travel far, and subsist long on a small Bag of it, taking only 6 or 8 Ounces of it per day, mix'd with water.—The Flour of Mayz, mix'd with that of Wheat, makes excellent Bread, sweeter, and more agreable than that of Wheat alone; To feed Horses, it is good to soak the Grain 12 Hours. They mash it easier with their Teeth, and it yields them more Nourrishment. The Leaves stript off the Stalks after the Grain is ripe, & ty'd up in Bundles when dry, are excellent Forage for Horses, Cows, &c. The Stalks pressed like Sugar Canes yield a sweet Juice, which being fermented and distill'd yields an excellent Spirit, boiled without Fermentation it affords a pleasant Syrop.—In Mexico, Fields are sown with it thick, that multitudes of small Stalks may arise, which being cut from time to time like Asparagus are serv'd in Deserts, and their sweet Juice [*pressed by the Teeth*] extracted in the Mouth, by chewing them.— The Meal wet is excellent Food for young Chickens, and the whole Grain for [large] grown Fowls. *Courtesy of the Library of Congress.*

Pour faire du Pain avec la Farine de Maïs, mêlée avec la Farine de Blé.

La Farine de Maïs demande plus de tems pour bien cuire, que la Farine de Blé; C'est pourquoi si on les mête à froid, et qu'on les fasse fermenter et cuire ensemble, la Partie de Blé sera suffisamment cuite, lorsque la Partie de Maïs sera encore crue.

Pour parer à cet inconvénient, Nous faisons bouillir un Pot d'eau dans lequel on jette un peu de Sel et pendant que l'eau bout, nous jetons dedans avec une main un peu de Farine de Maïs, et avec l'autre nous la remuons dans l'eau bouillante qu'on laisse sur le feu, et cette Opération doit être répétée avec un peu de Farine à chaque fois, jusqu'à ce que la Masse devienne si épaisse qu'on ait peine à la remuer avec le Baton. Ensuite, après l'avoir laissée quelque tems encore sur le feu, jusqu'à ce que la dernière Poignée ait bouilli, on l'ôte, et on verse la Masse dans la Huche, où on doit la bien mèler et pétrir avec une Quantité de Farine de Blé, suffisante pour former une Pâte propre à faire le Pain, et du Levain, ou de la Levure de Biére, pour la faire lever; et après le tems nécessaire on la met en Pains, et ensuite au Four.

To make Bread with Maize Flour mixed with Wheat Flour.

Maize Flour takes longer to bake well than Wheat Flour; so that if mixed together cold, then fermented and cooked, the Wheat part will be well baked whilst the Maize Part will remain uncooked.

To remedy this inconvenience, We boil one Pot of Water with a little Salt added and whilst the Water boils with one Hand we throw into it a little Maize Flour and with the other Hand stir it into the boiling Water that must be kept on the Fire, and this Operation shall be repeated with a little Flour each time, until the Mush is so thick it can hardly be stirred with the Stick. Then, after leaving it a little longer on the Fire, until the last Handfull has done boiling, it is taken off, then the Mush is poured into the Kneading Trough where it must be thoroughly mixed and kneaded with a Quantity of Wheat Flour sufficient to make a Dough thick enough to make Bread, and some Yeast, or Leaven, to make it rise; and after the necessary Time it is shaped into Loaves, and then put into the Oven. *Editor.*

Conversation with a Physician Who Long Lived in Russia.

July 3d./1782/

... The Russians have the art of distilling spirit from milk. To prepare it for distillation, it must, when beginning to sour, be kept in continual motion or agitation for twelve hours; it then becomes a uniform vinous liquor, the cream, curd, and aqueous part or whey, all intimately mixed. Excellent in this state for restoring emaciated bodies. This operation on milk was discovered long since by the Tartars, who in their rambling life often carry milk in leather bags on their horses, and the motion produced the effect. It may be tried with us by attaching a large keg of milk to some part of one of our mills (Smyth, X, 351).

A Letter from China.

Lisbon, May 5, 1784

... He liked their way of living, except their sometimes eating dog's flesh. Their pork was excellent; the rice, dressed various ways, all very good, and the *chong* he grew fond of, and learnt to make it. They put kidney beans in soak for twenty-four hours, then grind them in a hand mill, pouring in water from time to time to wash the meal from between the stones, which falls into a tub covered with a coarse cloth that lets the meal and water pass through, retaining only the skins of the beans; that a very small quantity of alum, or some sort of salt, put into it, makes the meal settle to the bottom, when they pour off the water. This is eaten in various ways, by all sorts of people, with milk, with meat, as thickening in broth, &c. (Smyth, IX, 204).

Such are the texts. Whether they were intended by Franklin for his cook, his friends or both is left to the imagination of the reader. A year ago the Philosophical Society gave a program entitled "Music enjoyed by Franklin." In a similar vein, these notes might have been entitled "Franklin's favorite dishes" for there is no doubt that the recipes represent the Doctor's own selection. It lies within the province of the biographers to decide whether they justify at least in part Brillat-Savarin's psycho-physiological conclusion: "Tell me what you eat and I'll tell you what you are."

www.ingramcontent.com/pod-product-compliance
Ingram Content Group UK Ltd.
Pitfield, Milton Keynes, MK11 3LW, UK
UKHW040659290326
469423UK00001B/5